# GERMANY

*Michael Burgan*

## W
## FRANKLIN WATTS
LONDON•SYDNEY

This edition 2012

First published in 2010 by
Franklin Watts
338 Euston Road
London NW1 3BH

Franklin Watts Australia
Level 17/207 Kent Street
Sydney NSW 2000

Copyright © Franklin Watts 2010, 2012

Produced for Franklin Watts by
White-Thomson Publishing Ltd
+44 (0) 843 208 7460
www.wtpub.co.uk

Series consultant: Rob Bowden
Editor: Sonya Newland
Designer: Clare Nicholas
Picture researcher: Amy Sparks

A CIP catalogue record for this book is available
from the British Library.

Dewey Classification: 943'.0883

ISBN 978 1 4451 0806 3

Printed in Malaysia

Franklin Watts is a division of Hachette Children's
Books, an Hachette UK company

www.hachette.co.uk

# Contents

# Introducing Germany

*Germany is one of the most powerful nations in Europe, with the largest economy and the second-largest population. The Germans are famous for their hard work and skill with advanced technology, and the country's great wealth makes it a world leader in economic and political affairs.*

## Where in the world?

Germany lies in the centre of Europe. It is bordered to the east by Poland and the Czech Republic. To the south are Austria and Switzerland. On Germany's western border lie France, Luxembourg, Belgium and the Netherlands. To the north is Denmark, as well as the North and Baltic Seas.

## A troubled past

For centuries, the area that is now Germany was made up of separate states ruled by dukes and princes. By 1871, many of these small German-speaking countries had united to form the German Empire. After World War I (1914–18), things were difficult for the German people but, in 1939, the German leader Adolf Hitler tried to expand the country's borders by invading other countries. This sparked World War II (1939–45), and led to the Holocaust – the killing of six million European Jews. Hitler also ordered the murder of five million other innocent people, including gypsies, Catholics and people with disabilities. Today, Germans and people around the world still try to understand how this event happened. They also try to make sure nothing like it ever happens again.

▲ *Germany's position in the heart of Europe has helped it become a powerful leader in areas such as trade and politics.*

4

## Building a new Germany

After losing the war, Germany was divided into two nations, West Germany and East Germany. West Germany became one of the world's strongest economies. East Germany came under the control of the communist Soviet Union, and the East German people had limited freedom. In 1989, the Soviet Union gave up its control and the two German nations soon reunited as a free country. Since then Germans have worked to overcome some of the problems of the past. The west still has many more people and a stronger economy, but all Germans are proud of their country and work to make it better.

### BASIC DATA

Official name: **The Federal Republic of Germany**

Capital: **Berlin**

Size: **357,022 sq km (134,847 sq miles)**

Population: **81,471,834**

Currency: **Euro**

▼ *The Brandenburg Gate in the capital Berlin was built in the 1800s as a symbol of peace.*

## World connections

Today, Germany is the wealthiest member of the European Union (EU), an association of 27 countries that work together on issues of trade, security and human rights, and is a world leader in international trade. Germany is also generous in aiding other nations. In 2009, it spent almost US$8 billion on foreign aid, and it plans to give more in the future.

## Language and people

Within Europe, Germany has a language link to several German-speaking lands around it, including Austria, Liechtenstein and Switzerland, where German is commonly spoken. Small groups of German-speakers also live in countries such as Belgium and Poland, and in Germany's former colonies in Africa, including Namibia and Rwanda. Over the centuries, Germans have also migrated to the USA, Canada and Brazil. The culture they brought – their language, food, religion and music – helped shape the growth of their adopted homelands.

▶ *The German influence can be seen in the architecture of many of its former colonies. This German-style church is in Windhoek, Namibia.*

▲ *Literacy rates are high in Germany – around 99 per cent of the population can read and write.*

## Looking ahead

Germany recovered more quickly than other European nations from the global recession that began in 2008. Its strong economy means Germany will continue to play an important role in international affairs. At home, the biggest challenge the country faces is a shrinking population. This means that German companies may need to find workers from overseas. Developing technology may help the country find ways of doing business with fewer workers, though, and this could help keep Germany strong.

### IT STARTED HERE

### Printing

Books were rare in Europe until a German called Johannes Gutenberg created a new printing process. The Chinese had already printed books, but during the 1450s, Gutenberg developed metal type and a press to print the type on to paper. These improvements made book printing much easier. Today, Germany publishes about 95,000 book titles each year, one of the highest rates in the world.

*With mountains to the south, two of the world's largest seas to the north, and forests and fields in between, Germany has a variety of landscapes. Some of the world's most famous rivers also wind across the country.*

## Highs and lows

The Alps mountain range runs through a small part of southern Germany and is the home of Zugspitze, the country's highest peak at 2,963 m (9,721 ft). Smaller mountains and hills surround the area, and the central part of Germany also has uplands that can rise to more than 1,000 m (3,280 ft). North Germany is much lower, with some stretches sitting below sea level. Germany has several islands in the north, situated in the Baltic and North seas.

▼ *Zugspitze stands on Germany's border with Austria. Snow covers the mountain for more than half the year, making it popular with skiers and snowboarders.*

## Forests

Around 30 per cent of Germany's land area is covered in forest, including the Black Forest in Baden-Wurttemberg. Over the centuries, people have cleared spruce, fir and pine trees there. In more recent years, pollution has killed large parts of the forest. Still, many trees remain and wood from some of them is used to make clocks that are famous around the world. Further east, the Bavarian Forest stretches into the Czech Republic, forming part of the largest continuous forest in Europe. Thuringia, in central Germany, has beech, spruce and pine forests that are well-known for their beauty.

▲ *Germany's forests are popular destinations for both German and foreign tourists, who enjoy hiking through the beautiful landscape.*

### PLACE IN THE WORLD

Total area: **357,022 sq km (134,847 sq miles)**

Percentage of world land area: **0.24%**

World ranking: **62nd**

## Waterways and lakes

The River Rhine – the longest river in Germany – actually begins in the Swiss Alps and also flows through France and the Netherlands before reaching the North Sea. The part of the Rhine that runs through Germany is the busiest waterway in Europe, as boats carrying both people and goods sail on it. Another river, the Elbe, was once part of the boundary between East and West Germany. Other important rivers include the Moselle, the Main, the Oder and the Ruhr. The country shares its largest lake, Lake Constance (Bodensee), with neighbouring Austria and Switzerland.

## IT'S A FACT!

Starting as a spring in south-west Germany, the Danube eventually becomes Europe's second-longest river, flowing for 2,776 km (1,725 miles). The river and the canals connected to it help link Germany with many neighbouring nations, forming a waterway that runs from the North Sea to the Black Sea.

▼ *The Rhine Valley is dotted with medieval castles, towns and villages. It is now a World Heritage Site.*

## Wildlife

Germany is home to a variety of wildlife. Wild boars and deer roam through some forests, and many kinds of water birds live along the country's lakes and rivers. Germany also has several endangered species, including the wildcat. Once found in many German states, only a few thousand of these cats exist today. The Germans have built bridges over some roads just for animals to use, hoping to keep cars from killing them.

▲ *Red deer roam throughout Germany's forests, even in the coldest winter months.*

## Climate

Most of Germany has a temperate climate: in most places the temperature does not drop sharply in winter or soar in summer. Areas closest to the North and Black seas tend to have warmer winters and cooler summers than the rest of the country. It can rain at any time, but rainfall tends to be higher during the summer. The areas around the Alps sometimes experience a warm wind off the mountains called a *foehn*.

## GOING GLOBAL

Millions of years ago, many different animals made their homes around a lake near Darmstadt in south-west Germany. The lake has gone, but fossils of the creatures remain. In the Messel Pit, people have found bones from prehistoric crocodiles, mammals, insects and fish. The pit is the world's best source for fossils from the Eocene period, which began about 57 million years ago. The Messel Pit is now a World Heritage Site.

# Population and migration

*With more than 80 million people, Germany has the largest population in Europe apart from Russia, which actually spans two continents. Despite the arrival of many immigrants, the German population is declining and it could soon be overtaken by other European countries.*

## The German people

The majority of Germans have roots in their homeland, and most live in the former West Germany, which was about twice as large as East Germany. One notable ethnic group is the Turks, at 2.4 per cent of the population. Other immigrants have come from Italy, Spain, Greece, Poland and Russia. Almost 75 per cent of the people live in cities or nearby urban areas. Berlin, the capital, is the largest city, with a population of 3.4 million. Other big cities include Hamburg, Munich, Cologne and Frankfurt, and several others have populations of more than 500,000.

▶ *Munich is the third largest city in Germany, with a population of around 1.3 million.*

## PLACE IN THE WORLD

Population: **81,471,834**

Percentage of world total: **1.17%**

World ranking: **16th**

## East and West

Since reunification, almost two million of the 16 million former East Germans have moved west. Most of them are well-educated young women seeking jobs in large cities. The people who remain in the east are mostly the elderly or young men without skills.

Some eastern cities have lost up to 30 per cent of their population since 1990. Some visitors to the east describe seeing empty homes, left by people who headed west. A much smaller number of Germans – from both the east and west – leave the country each year to look for work in other countries. Most head to other German-speaking countries such as Switzerland and Austria, but some settle further afield in countries such as the USA, which has attracted German immigrants for centuries.

*German-Americans march in a parade on Steuben Day in New York, USA.*

### IT'S A FACT!

Germany has five distinct minority groups. The Danes live mostly in Schleswig-Holstein, which once belonged to Denmark. The Friesians live near the Netherlands and the North Sea. The Sinti and Roma, traditionally nomadic, are spread throughout the country. The Sorbs live in eastern Germany. Each group has its own language, which the German government encourages them to use.

## A falling population

More and more people in Germany are deciding not to have children, or to have fewer children than in previous generations. This has led to a population decline across the country. Today, Germany has one of the lowest birth rates in the world. In 2007, the government began offering couples money so they could take more time off work to raise children. Still, the birth rate did not rise enough to stop the falling population.

## Immigration

During the 1950s and 1960s, West Germany welcomed immigrants from Turkey, Italy and other European nations. The newcomers were called *Gastarbeiters* – 'guest workers'. Most took low-paying jobs that the Germans did not want, and a lot of them made Germany their permanent home, raising families there. East Germany saw several different waves of immigrants from Vietnam. Some came to study then remained to begin careers, while others signed contracts to work there.

▶ *Despite efforts to encourage people to have more children, the birth rate in Germany is still slowing down. A falling birth rate means hospitals such as this one have plenty of room for newborn babies.*

### IT'S A FACT!

The German birth rate has declined steadily since the 1950s and is now the lowest in Europe, a position it shares with Italy. The birth rate is 8.3 births per 1,000 population. By comparison, the birth rate in France and the UK is 12.29, and in Spain it is 10.66.

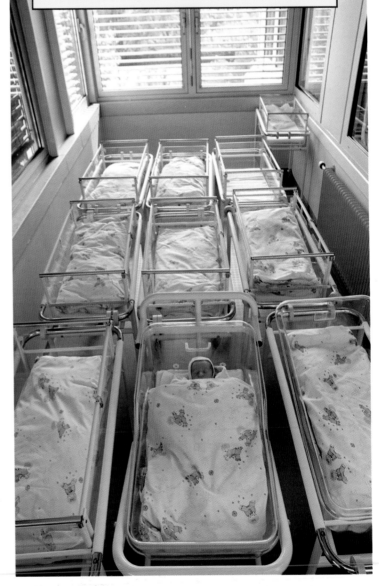

## Immigrants today

Since reunification, the number of immigrants to Germany has fallen from more than one million per year to around 721,000 in 2009. A lack of jobs has stopped the flow into the country, especially in the east. The Vietnamese are the largest immigrant group there, where many run their own restaurants and other businesses. Most new immigrants choose to settle in the west. In the cities of Stuttgart and Frankfurt, about 40 per cent of the population are foreign-born or the descendants of recent immigrants. In the east, Berlin has a large ethnic population. About 25 per cent of the residents have foreign roots.

▼ *Turkish shops and restaurants cater for the large Turkish population in Germany.*

### GOING GLOBAL

Immigration from Turkey has given Germany a Turkish flair. Some 800,000 Turks have taken German citizenship, and Turkish food can be easily found in large cities. As younger Turks become more comfortable speaking German, the government is encouraging them to continue to learn and speak Turkish, the country's second-most used language.

# Culture and lifestyles

*Germany has been the birthplace of many great thinkers, artists and writers, fuelled by one of the finest education systems in the world. Germans have also made technology a large part of their lives – the country has more Internet users than any other European nation.*

## A variety of religions

The Roman Catholic Church is one of several major Christian faiths in Germany, claiming more than 26 million members. In 2005, Joseph Ratzinger became the first German pope for almost 500 years, as Pope Benedict XVI. The Evangelical Church, a union of several smaller faiths, is the major Protestant religion. Germany's Jews once played a major role in the country's cultural life, but the rise of Hitler forced many to flee, and most of the others were killed. Fewer than 200,000 Jews live in Germany today. Muslims are a growing religious group, numbering close to four million.

### IT STARTED HERE

### The Protestant Reformation

In 1517, in the German city of Wittenberg, Martin Luther challenged the authority of the Roman Catholic Church, starting the Protestant Reformation. Catholics across Germany and other parts of Europe began to form new Christian religions that stressed the importance of following the Bible, not rules created by religious leaders. Luther's ideas led to the creation of Lutheranism, a Protestant faith that is now practised in dozens of countries.

▶ *German Pope Benedict XVI is the leader of the Roman Catholic Church. Around 34 per cent of Germans are Catholics.*

## A land of great ideas

Over the past few centuries, German philosophers such as Immanuel Kant and Friedrich Nietzsche have influenced people around the world. Karl Marx and Friedrich Engels helped create communism, a government system used today in several nations, including China. German scientists have also played major roles in world history. Wernher von Braun developed powerful rockets, while Max Planck helped create modern physics.

## Great writers

Germany's best writers are world famous, with their books translated into many languages. They include authors Hermann Hesse, Günter Grass and Thomas Mann. During the nineteenth century, brothers Jacob and Wilhelm Grimm collected and published German folktales. Such stories as *Snow White* and *Sleeping Beauty* are now read in more than 100 languages around the world.

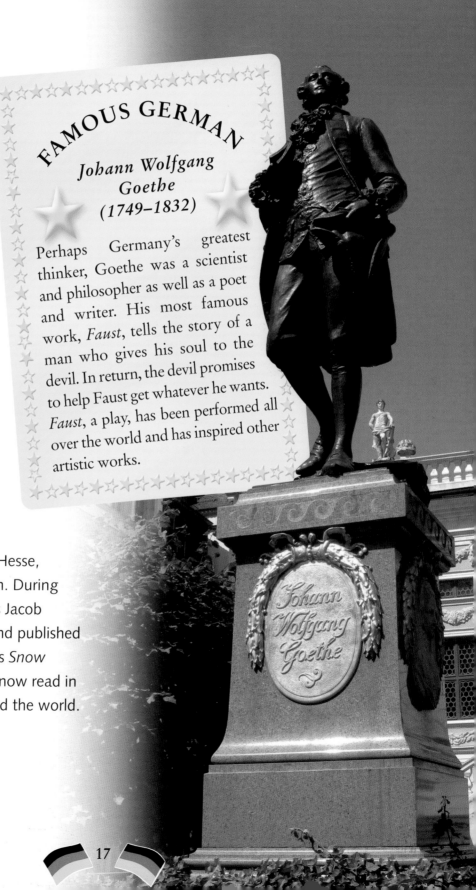

### FAMOUS GERMAN

#### Johann Wolfgang Goethe (1749–1832)

Perhaps Germany's greatest thinker, Goethe was a scientist and philosopher as well as a poet and writer. His most famous work, *Faust*, tells the story of a man who gives his soul to the devil. In return, the devil promises to help Faust get whatever he wants. *Faust*, a play, has been performed all over the world and has inspired other artistic works.

▶ *This statue of Goethe stands in Leipzig, where he spent three years studying law.*

17

▲ *The Berlin Philharmonic Orchestra was formed over 100 years ago and is now considered one of the best orchestras in the world.*

## Masters of music

Some of the world's greatest composers were German. Starting at the end of the eighteenth century, Ludwig von Beethoven wrote nine symphonies, as well as other pieces, that are still performed all over the world. In the nineteenth century, Richard Wagner wrote a series of operas called the *Ring* cycle, which are among the best-known operas of all time. In modern popular music, since the 1970s the band Kraftwerk has greatly influenced other artists with its use of electronic keyboards and drums.

### FAMOUS GERMAN

#### Johann Sebastian Bach
#### (1685–1750)

Born to a musical family in Thuringia, Bach was a church organist and composer. He wrote many pieces for keyboards, as well as works for both large and small musical groups. His most famous pieces include the *Brandenburg Concertos* and the *Goldberg Variations*. Modern musicians still perform Bach's music and sometimes borrow his melodies for their own works.

## The visual arts

Germany has had many fine artists whose works are displayed around the world. One of the first was Albrecht Dürer, who was known for his engravings of scenes from the Bible and everyday life. In more recent times, Germans have had a big influence on the development of cinema. In 1922, F. W. Murnau made the first vampire movie, *Nosferatu*. He later went to work in the USA, and his influence there helped develop the modern film industry.

## Sports

Germans love sports of all kind. They have excelled in football and events at both the Summer and Winter Olympic Games. Since the modern Games began in 1896, only two other nations have won more medals, counting the medals won when Germany was divided. Germany's Olympic Sports Association helps train more than 27 million athletes, both amateur and professional – more than any other national sports association. Great individual athletes include the skater Katerina Witt, tennis star Steffi Graf and Formula One racing car champion Michael Schumacher.

### IT STARTED HERE

#### Cinema

Two German brothers, Max and Emil Skladanowsky, were the first people to show movies to a paying audience. They invented a machine called the Bioskop, an early film projector. Their presentation took place in Berlin in 1895 and amazed the people who came to view it.

▼ *Michael Schumacher won the Formula One championship seven times between 1994 and 2004.*

▶ *Lena Schoeneborn of Germany celebrates a gold medal for the pentathlon at the 2008 Beijing Olympics.*

# Economy and trade

*Germany makes a variety of goods that are sold around the globe, helping to create the world's fifth-largest economy. More than half of Germany's exports are sold to other EU nations.*

## An advanced economy

Germany's BMW and the Daimler Group are just two German vehicle manufacturers. Together these car companies make Germany the world's fifth-largest car manufacturer. Germany is also a leading maker of electronic goods and communications technology, with Siemens an important company. The service industry makes up the largest part of the nation's economy, employing more than 28 million people. Service industries include banking, government, transportation and retail stores. To keep Germany's economy growing, both companies and the government spend billions of euros each year on research.

### IT STARTED HERE

#### Cars

In 1885, German inventor Karl Benz put a petrol-powered engine on a three-wheeled vehicle and created what is considered to be the world's first automobile. His company later became part of Mercedes Benz, owned by the Daimler Group.

▼ *A worker in a German BMW factory. Other famous German car manufacturers include Volkswagen and Porsche, and their vehicles are sold worldwide.*

## Farms and forests

Farming makes up only a small part of the German economy, yet German farms produce about 80 per cent of the country's food. Among EU nations, Germany is the leading producer of milk and pork, and among the leaders in beef, potatoes and grains. Leading food and drink exports include *wursts* (sausages) and cheeses. Germany also produces beer and wine, which are sold both at home and abroad. Germany's many forests provide wood used in a variety of ways. Lumber is used for building and trees also provide the raw material for paper.

## Natural resources

Germany's most important natural resources are iron, coal and potash, a chemical used in farming amongst other things. Germany's iron and coal are used to make steel. The country is one of the largest steel producers in the world, and the largest in Europe. The industry, however, suffered during the worldwide economic troubles of 2008–09, as did other German industries.

## GLOBAL LEADER

### Coal production

Germany produces more lignite – also called brown or soft coal – than any other nation. This type of coal is commonly used to generate electricity, and 24 per cent of Germany's electricity comes from power plants fuelled by lignite.

◄ *The Weisweiler power plant uses lignite to generate electricity, but there are concerns about the polluting gases released in the process.*

## Beyond Germany's borders

Germany was a founding member of the European Union and one of the first EU members to replace its own currency with the euro. With the largest economy in the EU, Germany's economic strength is important for the entire region. As part of the European Union, Germany is expected to help other European economies when they are in difficulty. In particular, their government has played a large part in helping the Greek government to function, after it slid into terrible debt difficulties. This has involved lending Greece huge amounts of money.

### FAMOUS GERMANS

*Karl (b. 1920) and Theo (1922-2010) Albrecht*

Theo Albrecht first sold groceries in his mother's small market. As an adult, he and his brother Karl launched their own grocery store, later called Aldi. The Albrechts sold fewer items and offered fewer services than other stores, but their prices were cheap. Over time Aldi added non-food items and opened more shops across Germany. Today the company has shops in many European nations, Australia and the USA. The Albrecht brothers became millionaires.

▼ German supermarket chain Aldi has spread throughout the world, with more than 1,000 stores in the USA alone.

## Global groups

Germany belongs to several international organizations that address world issues. At the same time, the member nations of these groups also watch out for their own interests. The Group of Eight (G8) holds meetings between the leaders of the world's eight largest industrial nations. Germany hosted the G8 in 2007. The Group of 20 (G20) includes nations that are quickly expanding their economies, such as Brazil, India and China.

### PLACE IN THE WORLD

| | |
|---|---|
| Value of economy: **US$2.94 trillion** | |
| Percentage of world total: **6%** | |
| World ranking: **6th** | |

## Trading partners

France is the top customer for German goods, followed by the USA and the UK. Eastern Europe and Asia are growing markets for German goods. Eastern Europe buys about 10 per cent of Germany's exports, and sales to China more than quadrupled between 2001 and 2011. For imports, Germany buys more goods from the Netherlands than from any other nation, followed by France and Belgium.

▼ *Container ships like this in the port of Hamburg – the third-largest port in Europe – are loaded with goods to be shipped all over the world.*

*The castles that dot Germany's landscape show the role royalty once played in ruling the people. Today, though, the government at all levels is democratic, as voters choose the people they want to represent them.*

## The Basic Law

The form of Germany's national government is outlined in the Basic Law. This document was written when West Germany was created in 1949. As part of the reunification process, East Germans agreed to follow the Basic Law. Under it, Germany has a federal system, which means that power is shared between the 16 German states and the national government. States make sure that both national and state laws are enforced, and since 2006 they have had greater control over issues such as education. Within the states, towns and cities have their own elected governments.

▲ *The Reichstag (parliament) building in Berlin. The words over the entrance mean 'For the German People'.*

### IT'S A FACT!

Germany's major parties are the Christian Democratic Union, the Christian Social Union, the Social Democratic Party, the Greens and the Left Party.

## Making laws

Every four years, voters elect representatives to the Bundestag, the German parliament, which creates Germany's national laws. Another body, the Bundesrat, also shapes the country's laws. The state governments elect its members, and they review all proposed bills and must approve certain ones before they become law. The Bundesrat also reviews issues related to Germany's role in the European Union.

## The role of parties

The Basic Law gives political parties specific roles in the government. The parties choose the people who run for office and organize their campaigns. In the Bundestag, the party with the most members chooses the chancellor, who is the leader of the national government. The chancellor selects the ministers who will head important government agencies, such as Defence, Health and Economics.

## GOING GLOBAL

Germany's Green Party was established in 1979, when Petra Kelly and others concerned about world peace and the environment launched their first campaign. Four years later, the party elected its first members to the Bundestag, including Kelly. Although other countries had environmentalist parties at the time, Kelly and the German Greens won global attention and inspired other Green Parties around the world.

◀ *The lower house of the German parliament – the Bundestag – in session.*

## Germany and the world

West Germany became a member of the North Atlantic Treaty Organization (NATO) in 1955 and both Germanys joined the United Nations (UN) in 1973. As a UN member, Germany promotes peace and human rights around the world. NATO is a military organization, and Germany has sent troops on several NATO missions, most recently to Afghanistan. After World War II, many Germans opposed their country's use of troops in foreign lands. Today, though, more Germans accept the country's role in certain wars.

### GOING GLOBAL

Each year, various non-profit groups send several thousand young adults around the world to help other nations. This is thanks to the German government's *Weltwaert* ('Worldwards') programme, which allows young Germans to help with projects such as caring for orphans in Africa or protecting rainforests in South America.

▼ *German troops – part of the NATO forces – in Afghanistan in 2009.*

## From enemies to friends

Germany has tried to build better relations with nations it had invaded during World War II, such as France, Poland and Russia. France and Germany now work closely on trade and defence issues. Poland is slowly improving its ties with Germany, thanks partly to increased trade. Russian and German leaders hold an annual meeting to seek stronger ties.

## A special foreign relationship

Soon after World War II, the nation of Israel was formed as a homeland for Jews. West Germany sought good ties with Israel, to make up for the suffering Hitler caused European Jews. That policy continues, and Germany has paid more than 26 billion euros to Israeli citizens who survived the Holocaust. German leaders have also tried to improve relations between Israel and its Arab neighbours, which have fought several wars since 1948.

▲ *German chanceller Angela Merkel meets with French prime minister Nikolas Sarkozy in 2009. The two countries now have close ties.*

### FAMOUS GERMAN

#### Konrad Adenauer (1876–1967)

Konrad Adenauer was elected West Germany's first chancellor in 1949. For almost 15 years, he helped repair Germany's relations with its former enemies and create a democratic government. Adenauer also helped restore social order, paving the way for Germany's great economic growth.

# Germany in 2020

*The world economic crisis hit Germany hard, as people lost jobs and cut back on spending. But Germany recovered more quickly than many other nations and is likely to remain one of the world's richest countries in the years ahead – even as it faces new problems.*

## Changes in the economy

Germany will move even more towards high-tech industries in the next decade, while traditional industries such as car-making may lose jobs to companies overseas. This change will bring a shift in population, as people move out of the areas that lose jobs and into the ones where new companies are growing. Germany will have lost its place as the world's top exporter to China, though other nations will still seek German goods.

▶ *Germany already has a world-renowned high-tech industry, but it is likely to grow in the coming years.*

## A shrinking population

Germany's population will be smaller in 2020, for a variety of reasons. Most young couples will continue to have few or no children, and more Germans will leave the country. Only immigration will help keep the population from shrinking even more. The population will also be older, thanks to improved healthcare and the reduced number of children. The government will struggle to pay for the needs of this larger elderly population. Immigrants will also face tough times. Germany may have trouble educating and providing other services such as healthcare for all the new arrivals.

## New sources of energy

The world will continue to fight global warming, and Germany is likely to play a key role. German engineers are already world leaders in technologies that reduce the use of fossil fuels, which worsen global warming. In 2020 about 25 per cent of the country's electricity will come from renewable energy sources such as wind and solar power. Germany plans to give up nuclear power by 2022 as a response to the Fukushima nuclear disaster in Japan.

▼ *A technician puts the finishing touches to the Lieberose Solar Park, which opened in April 2009.*

## GLOBAL LEADER

**Solar power**

The Lieberose Solar Park in Cottbus, Germany, was the world's second-largest solar plant when it was completed in 2009. The park covers an area equal to more than 210 football fields and produces enough electricity for 15,000 homes.

# Glossary

**colonies** territories under the immediate political control of a state.

**continent** one of the Earth's seven great land masses – Africa, Asia, Australia, Europe, North America, South America and Antarctica.

**democratic** a type of government where people vote for the people they wish to represent them.

**economy** the financial system of a country or region, including how much money is made from the production and sale of goods and services.

**engravings** art works created by digging out part of a material, such as wood or metal to form pictures.

**ethnic group** a group of people who identify with each other and feel they share a history.

**export** to transport goods or services to other countries for sale or trade.

**federal** a system of government with power shared between states and the national government.

**fossil fuels** fuels formed over millions of years from the remains of ancient life forms.

**global warming** the gradual rise in temperatures on the surface of the Earth, caused by changes in the amount of greenhouse gases in the atmosphere.

**high-tech** relating to electronics or sciences that rely on computers and other devices to produce goods.

**immigrants** people who have moved to another country to live.

**imports** to bring in goods or services to a country from other nations.

**migrate** to move to another country to live or work.

**minority** a relatively small group of similar people within a large population.

**natural resources** minerals, plants or other items from the earth or seas that are used to make products.

**philosophers** thinkers who study complex issues, such as the meaning of life and death, or how people should live together in society.

**pollution** spoiling the environment with man-made waste such as vehicle emissions, waste gases from factories, or chemicals from fertilizers.

**prehistoric** dating back before written history.

**Reformation** a movement, which began in Germany, that broke away from Catholicism and established the Protestant Church.

**reunification** the act of bringing back together two separate countries that were once one.

**symphonies** long musical pieces for orchestras, divided into three or four parts.

# Further information

## Books

*Germany (Celebrate!)*
by Robyn Hardyman
(Franklin Watts, 2009)

*Germany (Discover Countries)*
by Paul Harrison
(Wayland, 2009)

*Germany (Looking at Countries)*
by Kathleen Pohl
(Franklin Watts, 2008)

*Germany (The Changing Face of...)*
by Sonja Schanz
(Wayland, 2004)

*Nazi Germany (Questioning History)*
by Alex Woolf
(Wayland, 2008)

*Countries Around the World: Germany*
by Mary Colson
(Raintree, 2011)

## Websites

**https://www.cia.gov/library/publications/the-world-factbook/geos/gm.html**
CIA World Factbook – Germany. From the spy agency of the US government, this site includes a map and current statistics on Germany and its people.

**http://europa.eu/europago/welcome.jsp and http://europa.eu/youth**
These European Union sites have been set up especially for children and young people.

**http://www.tatsachen-ueber-deutschland.de/en/home1.html**
Sponsored by the German government, this site looks at the country's culture, economy and geography, among other topics, and offers links to other useful sites.

# Index

Numbers in **bold** indicate pictures